Until The Lion Learns To Tell
His Own Story, The Hunter Will
Always Be The Victor

AFRICAN PROVERB

Preface

This is the first of a two-volume book on selected Akan proverbs and their meaning. The proverbs make the wise wiser, it makes the primitive knowledgeable, and it increases the knowledge of the knowledgeable. The proverbs deepen a person's way of thinking. The Akan proverbs were originally recited at the Ashanti palace by qualified linguists who were handpicked by the king himself. The Ashanti king and the clan chiefs are the custodians of the Akan proverbs. Certain proverbs are recited depending on the occasion or the mood of the king. There are severe consequences for citing inappropriate or unsuitable proverbs in the presence of the king. Each proverb has a meaning but is open to various interpretations. The principles of the Akan proverbs are meant to be applicable to all regardless of nationality, heritage, or social standing.

Visual Context

Each page spread is laid out with an image on the left and a proverb (paired with an Adinkra symbol) on the right of the page. The images, mainly photographs, are not analogous to the proverbs, they are meant to provide insights into Ashanti and Ghanaian culture from a perspective that inspires pride. Each proverb is visually reinforced with an Adinkra symbol that shares similar meaning. The Adinkra symbols are proverbial pictographs that, like the proverbs, was commissioned and used by the king of the Ashantis. The hope is that this book will stimulate your interest, help you understand, not only the Ashantis but the people and the various cultures in Ghana as well.

SELECTED AKAN

PROVERBS

VOL 1

AND THEIR MEANING

Funtunfunafu Ne Dɛnkyɛmfurafu, Yafunu No Yɛ Baako Nanso Sɛ Wɔre Didi a Na Wɔre Fom

ALTHOUGH THE SIAMESE CROCODILES SHARE THE SAME STOMACH THEY COMPETE FOR FOOD

Although there is strength in numbers (in reference to a group of people), the individual contribution is integral to the success of the whole. The mythical Siamese crocodiles mentioned above are depicted in various Ashanti art forms including the famous Adinkra symbols.

Kɔtɔ Rewea Na Ne Ba Nso Rewea

BOTH THE GROWN CRAB AND THE BABY CRAB CRAWL

The parent struggles to make a living and the child struggles to survive. Everyone struggles whether old or young, rich or poor, good or bad, etc. At all stages in life, we are confronted with struggles and challenges.

Kɔtɔ Nnka Na Ne Nkyea Na Ɛyɛ Ya

THE CRAB DOES NOT BITE, BUT ITS HANDSHAKE IS PAINFUL

A duality usually exists between good and bad. For example, the same hand that feeds you can also be the one that leads to your demise. In other words, the gun that protects you could also be the one that takes your life. The fire that helps you cook your food can also destroy your home. In Western society, they say, "Live by the sword and die by it."

Kɔkɔsakyi De Ne Kwasea Pɛ Nyinkyere

FOR SAFETY AND SURVIVAL REASONS, THE VULTURE DELIBERATELY BEHAVES FOOLISHLY ON PURPOSE

The vulture is considered a fool because it scavenges on rotten food from the garbage dump, but it does so in order to decrease risk. The garbage dump is the last place to find a hunter. Also, the vulture increases its chances of survival by scavenging on the garbage dump because it faces little competition for food. Occasionally, unpopular decisions or actions are taken in order to avoid unfavorable outcomes.

Kɔkɔsakyi Kasa Kyerɛ Obonukyerefo a Ɔte No Abɛbuo Mu

THE VULTURE AND THE FOX COMMUNI- CATE IN PARABLES

There is an Ashanti fable about how the vulture caught the fox eating the carcass of its own mother, an act considered to be an abomination. The fox is now forced into a pact with the vulture and, to preserve their secret, the fox and the vulture communicates in parables. When or where a direct approach is not applicable, an indirect approach can be employed to achieve the goal. For example, in some cultures, women indirectly declare their love for men through action (body language), but not open dialogue.

Akɔ Ne Aba Ne Anwono

TO AND FRO (AS IN WEAVING) RESULTS IN GREAT DESIGN

It's the back and forth or to and fro movement of the weaver's hands that results in the creation of beautiful designs such as the Kente cloth. To be successful in life, one ought to work. Nothing is achieved without work.

Baabi a Ↄtomfoↄ Rebↄ Hↄ Panpan No Na ɛhↄ Hia

THE BLACKSMITH ONLY HAMMERS WHERE THE METAL REQUIRES FLA-TTENING OR SOFTENING

In solving a problem, the solution should be tailored to the problem. To heal the sick, treatment follows the diagnosis and not vice versa.

Ɔhene a Ɔnntie Afotuo No Natikɔ Pakyaa

THE KING WHO IGNORES ADVICE BEARS THE MARK OF DISGRACE AT THE BACK OF HIS HEAD

The king who refuses sound advice is mocked in his absence and faces humiliation alone. In short, a great leader is a great listener.

Ahoma a Eware No Na Ɛte Nkokɔ Bini

IT'S THE SPUN-OUT ROPE ON THE GROUND THAT COLLECTS (CHICKEN) EXCRETA

A person with no vision floats around without purpose. It may also mean, indisciplined people are predisposed to long-suffering.

Anantuo So Sene Ɛsrɛ a Na Yadeɛ Wo Mu

IT'S PROBLEMATIC FOR THE LEG TO BE LARGER THAN THE THIGH

It is abnormal or unusual for one's leg to be larger than the thigh. It's impossible for the eyeball to be bigger than the head. This means, in every society, there are abominations or taboos that ought to be adhered to.

Ekuro a Ɛbɛ Kum Kraman Ɛnna Ɛtɔ Napampam

THE WOUND ON THE DOG'S FOREHEAD IS THE ONE THAT ENDS IN ITS DEMISE

The dog licks its wounds to heal itself, but how does it heal the wound on its forehead if the tongue can't reach it? The wound on the dog's forehead becomes its undoing. For example, freezing the assets of the wealthy incapacitates them. In other words, the toothless and clawless lion ceases to be king of the jungle.

Dɛɛ Ɔrepɛ Adeɛ Akɔ Kɔtɔkɔ No Yɛnnyɛ No Abrɔ

A FELLOW ASHANTI IS NOT DENIED THE RIGHT TO BE PROSPEROUS

The proverb asks all Ashantis to be kind to each other, especially when living in a foreign land. An Ashanti helps another to succeed so all may succeed. In other words, the right hand washes the left hand and the left hand washes the right hand.

Sɛ Nwansena Annpa Efunu Aniase a Yɛde No Sie Efunu

THE STUBBORN FLY IS BURIED WITH THE CORPSE

In the face of a looming disaster, adhere to warnings and follow safety and security instructions. Those who disregard early warnings and instructions often face certain death or destruction. Another interpretation is, know when to quit.

NO LIFE

Sɛ Asuo Bi Kɔbɔ Asuo Bi Mu a Na Na No Adwo

THE STRENGTH OF THE STREAM IS DIMIN-ISHED AFTER ENTERING THE RIVER

The king bows to a greater king and they in turn answer to a higher authority. Your level of importance in society varies from place to place; you may be great in your land, but might be of little importance in another land.

Sɛ Woto Patraka Tuo Na Ɔse Kaa a, Ɔse Ɛka Dadaa

THE SOUND OF A GUNSHOT DOES NOT TAKE THE APE BY SURPRISE

Since hunting takes place in the forest and the Ape lives in the forest, it's used to the sound of gunshots. For example, an auto mechanic in greasy clothes is not a surprising sight. In Western society, they say, "it comes with the territory."

Twene a Yɛmmɔ Mu No Yɛnnhunu No Wɔ Efie

A FORBIDDEN DRUM IS NOT FOUND IN THE HOME

In the Akan (Ashanti) culture, the king may forbid certain drums from being played or owned by the citizenry. Therefore, those forbidden drums are not to be found in people's homes. Practices classified or deemed as taboo should be avoided at all cost.

Abusua Twene, Yɛde Ko–ntomire Ɛnna Ayere So

THE SURFACE OF THE DRUM CONST–RUCTED WITH COCOYAM LEAVES CAN ONLY BE BEATEN BY PARTICULAR MEMBERS OF THE CLAN

The surface of the drum constructed with cocoyam leaves, if it exists, would be extremely fragile and practically unbeatable except by a divinely gifted pair of hands or by persons with mythical playing skills. The moral of this proverb is, family issues are well handled by members of the family, but not an intruder. In any nation, the indigenous people enjoy privileges that are unavailable to foreign migrants.

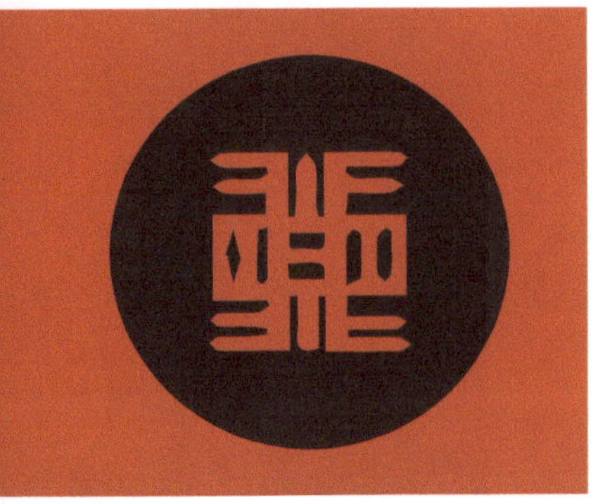

Obi Nnim a Obi Kyerɛ

IF ONE DOESN'T KNOW, ONE TEACHES

We learn from each other, so we must be willing to seek knowledge and teach with humility.

Sɛ Woto Pampim a Na Wato Kuro

ONE ENCOUNTERS THE DEFENSIVE WALL BEFORE ENTERING THE CITY

In life, the imminent danger is often preceded by several warning signs. Our actions are preceded by the decisions we make. For example, in the Akan (Ashanti) culture, a man has to perform marriage rites before marrying. No rites, no marriage.

Ɔhene a Ɔnni Abodin No Ɔnni Abɛntia

THE KING WITHOUT AN APPELLATION IS ONE WITHOUT A CEREMONIAL HORN

In the Akan (Ashanti) culture, the ceremonial horn is a symbol of the king's authority. The king without qualifi-cation (appell-ation) has no authority (ceremonial horn). For example, job seekers are asked to provide their credentials such as certifi-cates, diplomas, etc. in order to prove their qualifications.

Sɛ Wonsa Bɛware Anma Yɛatwa So Dɛɛ Fa Wonsa Tiaa Nante Ma Wasɛm Ntwa Tiawa Mma Wo

IT'S BETTER TO LIVE WITH A SHORT HAND THAN A LONG HAND THAT WOULD BE CUT SHORT

It's better to admit one's fault than to be later found guilty. It's better to quickly confess to crimes you commit than deny them. Denial only worsens the situation and prolongs the punishment.

Obi Nnfa Ne Nsa Benkum Nnkyerɛ Nagya Fie Kwan

NO ONE POINTS IN THE DIRECTION OF THEIR FATHER'S HOUSE WITH THEIR LEFT HAND

In the Akan (Ashanti) society, it's a taboo to use the left hand to gesture at people and certain objects in public. If a person is found doing that which is deemed a taboo, there must be a reason for such behavior. There are deep-rooted reasons why people misbehave.

Εmpaninfɔɔ Sε Εmoa Ndi Nkɔ, Deε Aka No Yεre Bɔ Ho Ban

IT'S BETTER TO PROTECT WHAT'S LEFT THAN CONCERN YOURSELF WITH THAT WHICH IS LOST

Sometimes, accept what's given and call it a day. One cannot control all things at all times. In the Western society, they say, "A bird in hand is better than two in the bush."

Akwadaa a Neyɛm Tuo Nnim Sɛ Wamo Danta

A PAIR OF DIAPERS IS NOT THE CURE FOR A CHILD WHO IS STRICKEN WITH DIARRHEA

When confronted with a problem, the core issues ought to be identified and thoroughly addressed in order to fix it. Always tailor the solution to the problem. Quick fix only creates additional problems. In other words, we should value our time and not waste it on frivolous, unworthy things. Also, avoid procrastination and address the most difficult problems.

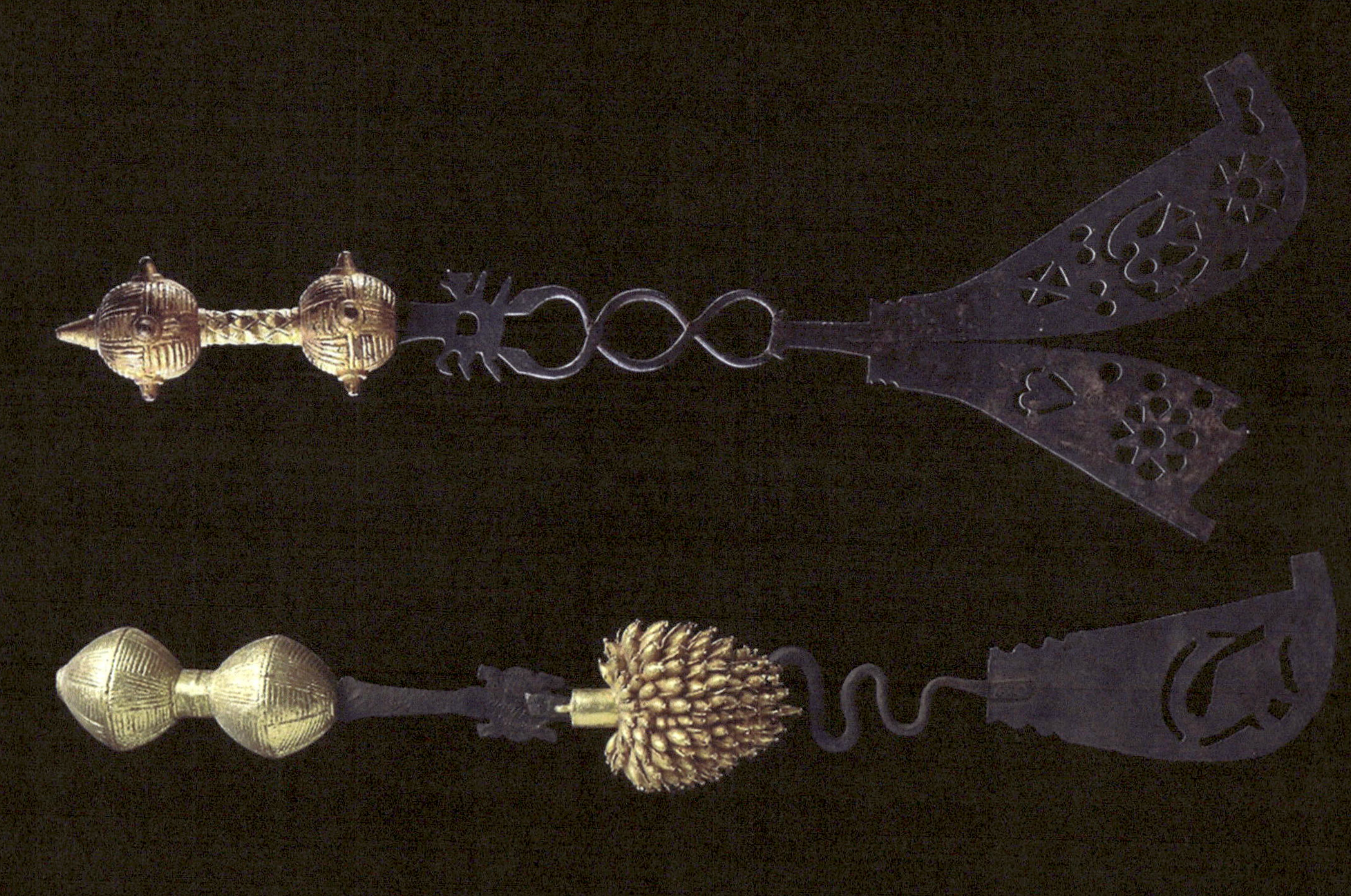

Humani So Ma Me Nti Na Atwe Mienu Nam

FOR THE SAKE OF HELPING EACH OTHER, THE ANTELOPE WALK IN PAIRS

This proverb reminds Ashantis of the power of the "whole", an integral value entrenched in the Akan society. In Western society, they say, "Two heads are better than one."

Wohuri Twa a Egu Wani So

WHEN YOU JUMP TO CUT A TREE BRANCH, YOU INVITE A SPECK INTO YOUR EYES

Accepting a job you are unqualified for only results in misery. Everything has a limit, so operate within your strength or capacity.

Akwadaa Huri Tra Ɔpanin a Ɔsa Ne Mmɛn Mu

WHEN A CHILD ATTEMPTS TO JUMP OVER AN ADULT, THE CHILD IS ENSNARED ON THE ADULT'S HORNS

The child that attempts what is meant for adults will suffer future consequences. Children are taught to abstain from behaviors or practices that are deemed, by society, to be beyond their understanding or (moral) maturity. Note that the "horns" mentioned above are an abstract or mythological concept and not to be taken literally.

Deɛ Ɔre Bobɔ Apɔ, Ɔmmɔ Mfa, Na Mmom Ɔrebɔ Agya Nkyirima

ONE WHO TIE KNOTS, IS NOT DOING SO FOR THEMSELVES ONLY, BUT ALSO FOR THEIR DESCENDANTS

This proverb addresses the unintended consequences of our evil actions. According to the proverb, the knots (evil plots) we tie for others (enemies) have ramifications that inadvertently sabotage our own loved ones. In other words, your actions today will impact your loved ones tomorrow, so refrain from creating generational problems.

Menkoara Metirimu Nso Ɛporɔ

KEEP YOUR KNOWLEDGE AND DIE WITH IT

Knowledge kept to oneself does not benefit anyone, especially when you die with it. There is a story of a man who kept the carcass of an antelope he had hunted in the bush, hoping to eat it all by himself, but subsequently fell ill and forgot to disclose the location of the meat to his family. He later recovered and rushed back to the bush only to discover the meat had rotted beyond consumption. This means selfish people are likely to lose their possessions.

Bosompo Ɛtrɛ Nanso Ɔbɛtoo Abotan

ALTHOUGH THE OCEAN IS MASSIVE AND POWERFUL, IT WAS PRECEDED BY THE ROCK

We always notice the long bushy beard, yet it was preceded by the eyebrow. Those who precede you in life are to be valued for their sacrifices and wealth of experience.

Ɛkwan Atware Asuo, Asuo Atwarɛ Kwan Ɔpanin Ne Hwan? Ɔpanin Ne Asuo, Asuo Fri Tete

THE ROAD CROSSES THE RIVER AND THE RIVER ALSO CROSSES THE ROAD—WHICH OF THEM HAS SENIORITY? THE SENIOR IS THE RIVER BECAUSE IT HAS EXISTED SINCE CREATION

Once in a while, the proverbs are delivered in a question-and-answer format like this one. This proverb reminds us of how nature was sequentially created; some beings preceded others for a good reason.

Ɔhɔhoɔ Enndi Abɛnkwan

THE STRANGER DOES NOT EAT
PALM NUT SOUP

Palm nut soup is a popular staple food in Ghana that owes its distinctive red color to the oil from the palm fruit. Palm nut soup, in combination with Fufu (boiled yam and cassava pounded into a starchy dough), is eaten with the hands or fingers. Since strangers usually have little or no change of clothes, they avoid the palm nut soup in order not to stain their clothes. This means one ought to obey the laws of a foreign land in order to avoid misfortune or mishaps.

Akɔkɔ Baatan Nan Tia Ɛban a Ennkum Ba

THE HEN MAY ACCIDENTALLY STEP ON ITS CHICKS, BUT HAS NO DESIRE TO KILL THEM

In the traditional Akan (Ashanti) society, children are punished in order to be edified, but not to intentionally inflict harm upon them. People who commit crimes are thrown into prison in order to reform them, not to have them exterminated. Another meaning is, our actions may have unintended consequences. Also, things are not what they seem to be.

Gye Meba Na Menfa Adeɛ Mmra a Na Ɛnnkyerɛ Sɛ Ɔde No Akyɛ Wo

TO ASK YOU TO HOLD MY BABY FOR ME DOESN'T EARN YOU THE RIGHT TO KEEP THE BABY FOR GOOD

Stay within your boundaries. Don't misuse any given power or authority. A caretaker position does not make you the owner of a house. Be humble and operate within the limits of your authority.

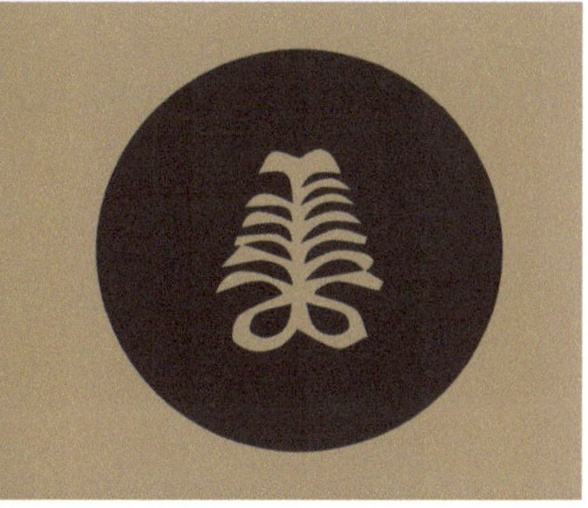

Abosomakotrɛ Ɛse Brɛbrɛw Yɛ, Ntɛm Nso Yɛ

THE MANTRA OF THE CHAMELEON IS, TO BE FAST IS GOOD AND TO BE SLOW IS ALSO GOOD

There is time for everything and, based on various factors, we choose to accelerate or reduce our pace.

Image List

1. The mythical siamese crocodiles; although they share the same stomach they fight for food.

2. Ghanaian girl looks up to the mother.

3. Ashanti gold headdress worn by page boys at the palace.

4. Cowbell – a three-beat note traditional music instrument.

5. An Ashanti drummer/announcer of messages or events (gold and bronze statue).

6. Kente weaver at his loom (Bonwire, Kumasi). Weavers either use shuttles, as seen in this picture, or their hands to pick the yarn.

7. Breastplate (Ashanti gold weight).

8. The totem of the Oyoko clan (clan of the Ashanti monarchy) is the eagle with an arm in its mouth to signify humility towards the remaining seven clans.

9. Soap (black soap) and body cream (shea butter) belonging to the Ashanti King.

10. Instead of a ring, women engaged to the Ashanti King are given this staff to hold in public.

11. Ghanaian seamstress cuts an African wax print fabric.

12. Tchaw Tchaw or Ohenema traditional sandals originally designed for and worn by the Ashanti King and Queen.

13. Adinkra stamps carved and ready for stamping.

14. A fishing town in Cape Coast, Ghana.

15. Cocoa pods on the tree.

16. Ashanti war drum. It mimics the roar of a leopard when the surface is stroked with a stick.

17. Fishia is the popular Ashanti architecture that means an enclosed or fortified house. The Adinkra symbol, Fihankra, was inspired by this architecture design.

18. Fishia is the popular Ashanti architecture that means an enclosed or fortified house. The Adinkra symbol, Fihankra, was inspired by this architecture design. Courtyard view.

19. Fishia is the popular Ashanti architecture that means an enclosed or fortified house. The Adinkra symbol, Fihankra, was inspired by this architecture design.

20. Cowries were used as a form of currency by the Ashantis and other cultures in pre-colonial sub-Saharan Africa.

21. Kente cloth—one of the original timeless designs.

22. Blacksmith removes an Adinkra (Gye Nyame) symbol wax cast from a clay mold.

23. Market woman scoops a handful of local Ghanaian berries.

24. Future generation; Ghanaian mother carries the child, hands-free, on her back.

25. Ashanti ceremonial swords.

26. Ghanaian men wearing traditional funerary cloth and Tchaw Tchaw or Ohenema (children of the king) sandals. Photo Credit: Felicia Abban.

27. Adinkrahene (chief of the Adinkra symbols) wooden stamp.

28. Photo of Ghanaian women, of Ashanti origin.

29. Bowls carved into the rock by slaves; the food received is proportional to the size of the hole carved by the slave.

30. The porcupine is the emblem of the Ashantis and the mascot of the revered football club, Kumasi Asante Kotoko.

31. Fetching water (gold and bronze statuettes).

32. Girl takes a stroll by the beach in Accra.

33. Women dressed in matching Adinkra motif cloth.

34. Alasa fruit is a seasonal Ghanaian snack. The seeds are used in a famous local game.

35. The Calabash is synonymous with the palm–wine and the palm–wine brings everyone together.

Glossary

Akan (ah-kan) — people of ethnicity and origin found in mid-Ghana, West Africa. The Ashantis are the most famous Akans. The Akan people comprise the following subgroups: Ashanti, Abinghi, Abbe, Abidji, Aboure, Adjukru, Ahafo, Ahanta, Akuapem, Akwamu, Akye, Akyem, Alladian, Anyi, Aowin, Assin, Attie, Avatime, Avikam, Baoulé, Abron, Chokosi, Denkyira, Ehotile, Evalue, Fante, Kwahu, M'Bato, Nzema, Sefwi, Tchaman, Twifu and Wassa Jwira Pepesa. Akans can be found in countries such as Ivory Coast, Seychelles Island, Surinam, Brazil, etc.

Ashanti (ash-anti) — also known as Asante (ah-san-tee). Ashantis are Akans with origins from present–day central Ghana, West Africa. The Ashanti kingdom is still intact and powerful today. Ashantis are steeped in tradition, customs, rich in history, and known for pomp and pageantry. The name Asante is synonymous with war, they are known for their long history of wars, they are war-like people.

Kente (ken–tay) — brightly colored handwoven fabric with origins from the Ashanti town of Bonwire. The name Kente is derived from the Twi name for basket. It also refers to the alternating rhythmic (open and press) motion made by the loom. Kente is traditionally called "Nwentoma", which means, woven cloth.

Twi (chwee) — a dialect of the Akan language spoken by the Ashantis from Ghana, West Africa. Twi is the widely spoken language in Ghana.

Fufu (fuu-fu) — starchy (cassava and plantain) staple food common in most West African countries is popular among the Ashantis.

Akan Alphabet

Aa(ah)   **Bb**(beh)   **Dd**(deh)   **Ee**(aay)   **Ɛɛ**(eh)   **Ff**(fu)   **Gg**(geh)   **Hh**(huh)

Ii(eee)   **Kk**(keh)   **Ll**(ill)   **Mm**(mmm)   **Nn**(inn)   **Oo**(oh)   **Ɔɔ**(or)   **Pp**(pah)

Rr(rrh)   **Ss**(sss)   **Tt**(tsi)   **Uu**(uh)   **Ww**(weh)   **Yy**(yeh)

Democracy
Endurance
Courage
Ingenuity
Agreement
Commitment
Fortitude
Cooperation
Independence
Greatness
Security
Wisdom
Loyalty
Strength
Adaptability
Imprisonment
Friendship
Learn From The Past
Perseverance
Intelligence

ADINKRA SYMBOLS

Beauty

Initiative

Democracy

Vigilance

Supremacy

Peace

Guardianship

Knowledge

Examination

Divine Protection

Mortality

Faithfulness

Nurturing

Reconciliation

Resourcefulness

Acknowledgements

Special thanks to William Lomax and Marita Rivero for taking the time to review and edit the drafts. We couldn't have arrived at this polished material without your fundamental understating of the proverbs, great command of the English language, and attention to detail. Thank you!

"Thanks to my son, Nartey Kojo Odonkor, for inspiring me to share the history and culture of my Ghanaian and African ancestry with him and many other multi-nationals/culturals worldwide." _(Maté Naté)

"My sincere thanks go to my late Principal, Mr. Boadi of Assin Akonfudi, my younger brother, educationist, and chief linguist of Banko–Asante, Nana Adjeibi Frimpong, my wife Obaapa Adwoa Nyakoma and our children for their unconditional love and support. Thanks to the Yenkassa organization for exposing me and my work (what the creator has planted in me) to a wider global audience." _(Kwame Frimpong Manso Adakabre)

KWAME FRIMPONG MANSO ADAKABRE

CHIEF LINGUIST

Kwame Frimpong Manso Adakabre is an Akan, an Ashanti. He was trained in Akan tradition and customs and has been the chief linguist for his family head for the past 30 years. He was picked to be a linguist because of his lineage and fluency in the Akan language and customary devices. He is the author of works of literature on Akan culture. This book is a testament to Kwame Frimpong Manso Adakabre's resolve to fulfill his life goal of leaving footprints for the younger generation to follow.

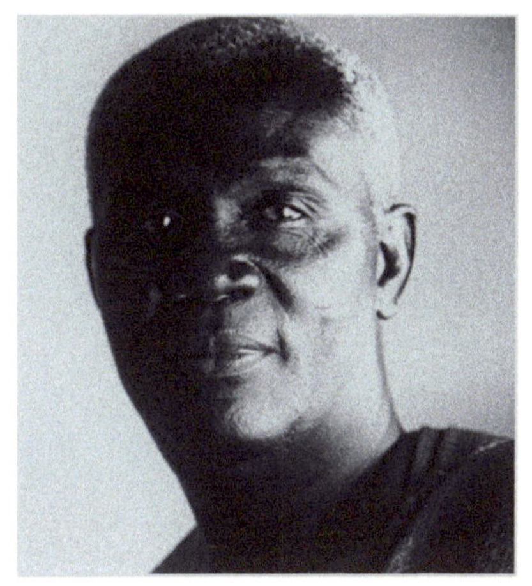

MATÉ NATÉ

FOUNDING DIRECTOR, YENKASSA

Maté Naté is an avid student of history, a native of Ghana but currently lives in Los Angeles, USA. He is a User Experience Designer who holds a BFA in Graphic Design from Massachusetts College of Art & Design (Massart), MFA in Digital Media from Rhode Island School of Design (RISD), and a Collegiate Teacher's Certificate from Brown University. Maté Naté has designed software and online experiences for companies and organizations such as Oracle, Fidelity Investments, AthenaHealth, and PBS. Maté Naté is the founder and director of Yenkassa, an organization that seeks to collect and share stories from older generation Sub-Saharan Africans.